Classic Wisdom

— for the —

PROFESSIONAL LIFE

CLASSIC WISDOM

—— FOR THE ——

PROFESSIONAL LIFE

EDITED BY

BRYAN CURTIS

THOMAS NELSON
Since 1798

NASHVILLE DALLAS MEXICO CITY RIO DE JANEIRO

Published in Nashville, Tennessee, by Thomas Nelson. Thomas Nelson is a registered trademark of Thomas Nelson, Inc.

Page design by Stacy Clark

Thomas Nelson, Inc., titles may be purchased in bulk for educational, business, fund-raising, or sales promotional use. For information, please e-mail SpecialMarkets@ThomasNelson.com.

Library of Congress Cataloging-in-Publication Data

ISBN 978-1-59555-126-9

Printed in the United States of America
08 09 10 11 12 WOR 6 5 4 3 2 1

To Kelly

The Professional Life

It really is true.

Once you get out of school, you will spend more hours working than almost any other thing you do. You will work more hours than you eat, watch television, or probably even sleep.

One very important lesson I learned a long time ago is that if you are going to spend eight or more hours, five or more days a week doing something, you better enjoy doing it. And it also helps if along the way you get good at doing it. That is the message of this book—find something you love doing and get good at it.

Some of you will receive this book as a gift. Maybe you just graduated from college and a loved one wrapped this book up and presented it to you. I hope they also included a nice check or a gift card. But even if there was no cash with the book, you are still lucky. You have someone in your life who wants you to succeed and be happy. Those are some pretty big shoulders you can climb onto as you begin your professional life.

Some of you purchased this book with the wages of your labor. In this case the lucky person or persons are your employers and/or employees. Anyone who wants to improve their professional skills—be it leadership skills, communication skills, or even listening skills, will be both a better boss and a better worker. Isn't it great when your boss is also a good worker?

Maybe you are trying to get the courage to start your own business. Maybe you are trying to become a better worker so you can get that promotion and earn more money. Or maybe you are just looking for some positive reinforcement—that you deserve to enjoy your job.

But however you received this book, I hope you will spend some time with it and pay heed to the advice you read here. Some of it comes from ancient scholars. Some of it comes from business professionals have made billions of dollars. And some comes from the people who make you laugh on cable. But I believe that if you are looking for the motivation that will help make your professional life a happier and more successful one, you will find something here you can use.

Find one quote or 101 quotes in this book that speak to you. Read them when you need a boost or an injection of wisdom, and then go use that wisdom to make your professional life just one aspect of a simply amazing life.

CLASSIC WISDOM

——FOR THE——

PROFESSIONAL LIFE

the
professional
life

Love what you do. Get good at it.
Competence is a rare commodity
in this day and age.

JON STEWART

Coming together is a beginning.
Keeping together is progress.
Working together is success.

HENRY FORD

What I know is, is that if you
do work that you love, and the work
fulfills you, the rest will come.

OPRAH WINFREY

The key to longevity is to keep doing what you do better than anyone else. We work real hard at that. It's about getting your message out to the consumer. It's about getting their trust, but also getting them excited, again and again.

RALPH LAUREN

Know and accept your own strengths and weaknesses. In other words: Look at yourself honestly . . . understand your passions, your skills, your temperament, and your limitations. If you're a square peg, no matter how hard you—and others—try, you're just not going to fit very well into a round hole.

KATIE COURIC

It's important to scare yourself,
to do things you don't think
you're capable of doing.

REESE WITHERSPOON

It takes 20 years to build a reputation
and 5 minutes to ruin it. If you think
about that you will do things differently.

WARREN BUFFETT

To love what you do and feel
that it matters—how could
anything be more fun?

KATHARINE GRAHAM

I think the one lesson
I have learned is that there is
no substitute for paying attention.

DIANE SAWYER

The true measure of a career is
to be able to be content, even proud,
that you succeeded through
your own endeavors without leaving
a trail of casualties in your wake.

ALAN GREENSPAN

There is no failure. Only feedback.

ROBERT ALLEN

■ ■ ■ ■ ■ ■ ■ ■

The fastest way to succeed is
to look as if you're playing by
somebody else's rules, while
quietly playing by your own.

MICHAEL KORDA

■ ■ ■ ■ ■ ■ ■ ■

One person with passion is better
than forty people merely interested.

E. M. FORSTER

I wasn't running toward the theater
but running away from the sporting goods
store. Of course now that I'm selling
spaghetti sauce (with Newman's Own),
I begin to understand the romance
of business, the allure of being the
biggest fish in the pond and the juice you
get from beating out your competitors.

PAUL NEWMAN

It's hard to beat a person
who never gives up.

BABE RUTH

How many cares one loses
when one decides not to be
something but to be someone.

COCO CHANEL

You can't get people excited
unless you can help them
see and feel the impact.

BILL GATES

The imagination is how things get done.
You have to cultivate creativity.

RUSSELL SIMMONS

Few things can help an individual
more than to place responsibility on him,
and to let him know that you trust him.

BOOKER T. WASHINGTON

■ ■ ■ ■ ■ ■ ■ ■

If you are going to achieve
excellence in big things,
you develop the habit
in little matters. Excellence
is not an exception, it is
a prevailing attitude.

COLIN POWELL

■ ■ ■ ■ ■ ■ ■ ■

The man who does not work for the love
of work but only for money is not likely
to make money nor find much fun in life.

CHARLES SCHWAB

A person should set his **goals** as early as he can and **devote** all his energy and talent to getting there. With enough effort, he may achieve it. Or he may find something that is even more **rewarding**. But in the end, no matter what the outcome, he will know he has been alive.

WALT DISNEY

Learn young about hard work
and manners—and you'll be through
the whole dirty mess and nicely
dead again before you know it.

F. SCOTT FITZGERALD

■ ■ ■ ■ ■ ■ ■ ■

The person who makes
a success of living is the one
who sees his goal steadily
and aims for it unswervingly.
That is DEDICATION.

CECIL B. DEMILLE

■ ■ ■ ■ ■ ■ ■ ■

There is no man living who isn't capable
of doing more than he thinks he can do.

HENRY FORD

Life is to be lived. If you have to support yourself, you had bloody well better find some way that is going to be interesting. And you don't do that by sitting around wondering about yourself.

KATHARINE HEPBURN

■ ■ ■ ■ ■ ■ ■ ■

Note how good you feel after you have encouraged someone else. No other argument is necessary to suggest that one never miss the opportunity to give encouragement.

GEORGE ADAMS

Great works are performed not
by strength but by perseverance.

Samuel Johnson

It's a good thing to turn your mind upside
down now and then, like an hourglass,
to let the particles run the other way.

Christopher Morley

Hire character. Train skill.

Peter Schutz

Think like a wise man but communicate
in the language of the people.

William Butler Yeats

My philosophy of life is that
if we make up our mind what we
are going to make of our lives, then
work hard toward that goal, we never
lose—somehow we win out.

If you're walking down the right
path and you're willing to keep walking,
eventually you'll make progress.

Sometimes you will apply for a job and
you won't get it and you will think it is
the greatest setback, but just remember
it isn't losing that is wrong; it is quitting.
Don't quit. Don't ever quit. Keep trying,
because this country needs the very
best that you, the young generation
of America, can give to it.

RICHARD NIXON

Every organization should
tolerate rebels who tell the
emperor he has no clothes.

COLIN POWELL

Whenever you are asked if you can do
a job, tell 'em, "Certainly, I can!"

THEODORE ROOSEVELT

Really big people are, above everything else, courteous, considerate and generous—not just to some people in some circumstances—but to everyone all the time.

THOMAS J. WATSON

Confidence, like art, never comes from having all the answers; it comes from being open to all the questions.

EARL GRAY STEVENS

If you don't find a way to do something as work that is fulfilling and enjoyable, then your life is going to be really sad.

RUDY GIULIANI

It's kind of fun to do the impossible.

WALT DISNEY

By failing to prepare you are preparing to fail.

BENJAMIN FRANKLIN

It's not the will to win that matters—everyone has that. It's the will to prepare to win that matters.

PAUL "BEAR" BRYANT

Keep away from people who try

to belittle your ambitions. Small people

always do that, but the really great make

you feel that you, too, can become great.

MARK TWAIN

Success seems to be connected with action. Successful people keep moving. They make mistakes, but they don't quit.

CONRAD HILTON

Keep on going and the chances are you will stumble on something, perhaps when you are least expecting it. I have never heard of anyone stumbling on something sitting down.

CHARLES F. KETTERING

Always be a first-rate version of yourself, instead of a second-rate version of somebody else.

JUDY GARLAND

When we are doing what we love, we don't care about time. For at least at that moment, time doesn't exist and we are truly free.

MARCIA WIEDER

All labor that uplifts humanity has
dignity and importance and should be
undertaken with painstaking excellence.

Dr. Martin Luther King Jr.

When your work speaks
for itself, don't interrupt.

Henry J. Kaiser

The difference between perseverance and obstinacy is that one comes from a strong will, and the other from a strong won't.

Henry Ward Beecher

The only way to get people to like working hard is to motivate them. Today, people must understand why they're working hard. Every individual in an organization is motivated by something different.

Rick Pitino

You only get out of it what you put into it. If you are a sheep in this world, you're not going to get much out of it.

Greg Norman

Quality is not an act. It is a habit.

ARISTOTLE

■ ■ ■ ■ ■ ■ ■ ■

Your success in life isn't based on your ability to simply change. It is based on your ability to change faster than your competition, customers, and business.

MARK SANBORN

■ ■ ■ ■ ■ ■ ■ ■

In the end, the customer doesn't know, or care, if you are small or large as an organization . . . she or he only focuses on the garment hanging on the rail in the store.

GIORGIO ARMANI

Confidence and enthusiasm are the greatest sales producers in any kind of economy. Have confidence in your products and the house backing them, have enthusiasm for your job, call on your trade regularly and consistently, treat your trade courteously, and you will find that your customers will not have to be sold—they will be glad to buy.

O. B. SMITH

■ ■ ■ ■ ■ ■ ■ ■

Courage is the main quality of leadership, in my opinion, no matter where it is exercised. Usually it implies some risk—especially in new undertakings. Courage to initiate something and to keep it going, pioneering and adventurous spirit to blaze new ways, often, in our land of opportunity.

WALT DISNEY

The very essence of leadership is that you have to have a vision.

THEODORE HESBURGH

Even a correct decision is wrong
when it was taken too late.

LEE IACOCCA

The highest reward for a person's
toil is not what they get for it,
but what they become by it.

JOHN RUSKIN

Wherever smart people work,
doors are unlocked.

STEVE WOZNIAK

The dictionary is the only place that success comes before work. Hard work is the price we must pay for success. I think you can accomplish anything if you're willing to pay the price.

Vince Lombardi

The older I get, the more I see
a straight path where I want to go.
If you're going to hunt elephants,
don't get off the trail for a rabbit.

T. Boone Pickens

In a time of drastic change,
it is the learners who inherit
the future. The learned find
themselves equipped to live in
a world that no longer exists.

Eric Hoffer

You've got to look for a gap,
where competitors in a market have
grown lazy and lost contact with
the readers or the viewers.

Rupert Murdoch

You will never make a good leader unless you have learned to follow. On those initial journeys when you are asked to pull your oar while another leads, learn what it takes to be a team player. Learn how to get along with others. Learn what loyalty and honesty are all about.

Dr. Robert Ballard

Above all, we wish to avoid having a dissatisfied customer. We consider our customers a part of our organization, and we want them to feel free to make any criticism they see fit in regard to our merchandise or service. Sell practical, tested merchandise at reasonable profit, treat your customers like human beings— and they will always come back.

L. L. Bean

The reward for work well done is the opportunity to do more.

JONAS SALK

Success is a lousy teacher. It seduces smart people into thinking they can't lose.

BILL GATES

What is it that you like doing? If you don't like it, get out of it, because you'll be lousy at it.

LEE IACOCCA

We all have a tendency to use research as a drunkard uses a lamppost—for support, but not for illumination.

DAVID OGILVY

A salesman minus enthusiasm
is just a clerk.

HARRY F. BANKS

If you do build a great
experience, customers tell
each other about that. Word
of mouth is very powerful.

JEFF BEZOS

Doing business without advertising
is like winking at a girl in the dark.
You know what you are doing,
but nobody else does.

STEUART HENDERSON BRITT

I think we consider too much the good luck of the early bird and not enough the bad luck of the early worm. I'm not the smartest fellow in the world, but I can sure pick smart colleagues.

Franklin D. Roosevelt

If you have a job without any aggravations, you don't have a job.

Malcolm S. Forbes

The test of a **successful** person is not an ability to eliminate all problems before they arise, but to meet and work out difficulties when they do arise. We must be **willing** to make an intelligent **compromise** with perfection lest we wait forever before taking action. It's still good advice to cross bridges as we come to them.

DAVID JOSEPH SCHWARTZ

All you need is love . . . and some
comprehensive technology!

BONO

■ ■ ■ ■ ■ ■ ■ ■

Harshness to me is giving somebody
false hopes and not following
through. That's harsh. Telling some
guy or some girl who've got zero
talent that they have zero talent
actually is a kindness.

SIMON COWELL

■ ■ ■ ■ ■ ■ ■ ■

Use power to help people. For we are
given power not to advance our own
purposes nor to make a great show in the
world, nor a name. There is but one just
use of power and it is to serve people.

GEORGE W. BUSH

Never continue in a job you don't enjoy. If you're happy in what you're doing, you'll like yourself, you'll have inner peace. And if you have that, along with physical health, you will have had more success than you could possibly have imagined.

JOHNNY CARSON

I am a great believer in luck,
and I find the harder I work,
the more I have of it.

THOMAS JEFFERSON

Leadership is action, not position.

DONALD H. MCGANNON

Before anything else, preparation
is the key to success.

ALEXANDER GRAHAM BELL

The future belongs to people who see
possibilities before they become obvious.

TED LEVITT

The absolute fundamental aim is to make money out of satisfying customers.

JOHN EGAN

■ ■ ■ ■ ■ ■ ■ ■ ■

The secret of joy in work is contained in one word—excellence. To know how to do something well is to enjoy it.

PEARL BUCK

■ ■ ■ ■ ■ ■ ■ ■ ■

If your actions create a legacy that inspires others to dream more, learn more, do more, and become more, then you are an excellent leader.

DOLLY PARTON

Nearly every man who develops an idea works at it up to the point where it looks impossible, and then gets discouraged. That's not the place to become discouraged.

THOMAS EDISON

Nothing can stop the man with the right mental attitude from achieving his goal; nothing on earth can help the man with the wrong mental attitude.

THOMAS JEFFERSON

Don't fight a battle if you don't gain
anything by winning.

GEORGE S. PATTON

Far and away the best prize that
life has to offer is the chance to
work hard at work worth doing.

THEODORE ROOSEVELT

There is no security in life,
only opportunity.

MARK TWAIN

The essential question is not, "How busy are you?" but "What are you busy at?" "Are you doing what fulfills you?"

OPRAH WINFREY

■ ■ ■ ■ ■ ■ ■ ■ ■

To turn really interesting ideas and fledgling technologies into a company that can continue to innovate for years, it requires a lot of disciplines.

STEVE JOBS

■ ■ ■ ■ ■ ■ ■ ■ ■

In the business world, everyone is paid in two coins: cash and experience. Take the experience first; the cash will come later.

HAROLD GENEEN

Modesty is a virtue that can never thrive in public. . . . A man must be his own trumpeter. He must get his picture drawn, his statue made, and must hire all the artists in his turn, to set about the works to spread his name, make the mob stare and gape, and perpetuate his fame.

JOHN ADAMS

An expert is a man who has
made all the mistakes, which can
be made in a very narrow field.

NIELS BOHR

Paying attention to simple little
things that most men neglect
makes a few men rich.

HENRY FORD

It is easier to go down
a hill than up, but the view
is best from the top.

ARNOLD BENNETT

You don't get paid for the hour. You get
paid for the value you bring to the hour.

KAREEM ABDUL-JABAR

People underestimate their capacity for change. There is never a right time to do a difficult thing. A leader's job is to help people have vision of their potential.

JOHN PORTER

■ ■ ■ ■ ■ ■ ■ ■

What we really want to do is what we are really meant to do. When we do what we are meant to do, money comes to us, doors open for us, we feel useful, and the work we do feels like play to us.

JULIA CAMERON

Respect your fellow human being, treat them fairly, disagree with them honestly, enjoy their friendship, explore your thoughts about one another candidly, work together for a common goal and help one another achieve it. No destructive lies. No ridiculous fears. No debilitating anger.

BILL BRADLEY

I don't design clothes, I design dreams.

RALPH LAUREN

∎ ∎ ∎ ∎ ∎ ∎ ∎ ∎ ∎

Your most unhappy
customers are your greatest
source of learning.

BILL GATES

∎ ∎ ∎ ∎ ∎ ∎ ∎ ∎ ∎

All good businesses are personal.
The best businesses are very personal.

MARK CUBAN

Don't be afraid to give your best
to what seemingly are small jobs.
Every time you conquer one it makes
you that much stronger. If you do
the little jobs well, the big ones will
tend to take care of themselves.

WILLIAM PATTEN

Trust your own instinct. Your mistakes might as well be your own, instead of someone else's.

BILLY WILDER

When work is a pleasure, life is joy!
When work is a duty, life is slavery.

MAXIM GORKY

No man ever listened himself out of a job.

CALVIN COOLIDGE

The only disability in life is a bad attitude.

SCOTT HAMILTON

The genius of a good leader is to leave behind him a situation which common sense, without the grace of genius, can deal with successfully.

Walter Lippmann

Know your power and follow your passion. The power and passion that spring from the beauty of your dreams, the depth of your imagination, and the strength of your values.

Nancy Pelosi

There are few, if any, jobs in which ability alone is sufficient.
Needed, also, are loyalty, sincerity, enthusiasm, and team play.

WILLIAM B. GIVEN JR.

You should recognize that criticism is not always a put down. If you take it to heart, maybe it will guide the way you ought to be going.

JOSEPH FLOM

There is no indispensable man.

WOODROW WILSON

Going to work for a large company is like getting on a train. Are you going sixty miles an hour or is the train going sixty miles an hour and you're just sitting still?

J. Paul Getty

■ ■ ■ ■ ■ ■ ■ ■

When you get a chance to earn a living, living your dream, you cannot beat that. So if that happens for you, embrace that with your entire being.

Smokey Robinson

Only when the human spirit is allowed to invent and create, only when individuals are given a personal stake in deciding economic policies and benefiting from their success—only then can societies remain economically alive, dynamic, progressive, and free.

RONALD REAGAN

Nothing will work
unless you do.

MAYA ANGELOU

Of course, you can't gain ground
if you are standing still.

BILL CLINTON

It is awfully important
to know what is and what
is not your business.

GERTRUDE STEIN

Labor disgraces no man, but
occasionally men disgrace labor.

ULYSSES S. GRANT

Success is not measured by what a man accomplishes, but by the opposition he has encountered and the courage with which he has maintained the struggle against overwhelming odds.

CHARLES LINDBERGH

■ ■ ■ ■ ■ ■ ■ ■ ■

Don't let the fear of the time it will take to accomplish something stand in the way of your doing it. The time will pass anyway; we might just as well put that passing time to the best possible use.

EARL NIGHTINGALE

I do not think that there is any
other quality so essential to success
of any kind as the quality of
perseverance. It overcomes almost
everything, even nature.

John D. Rockefeller

Winning is important to me,
but what brings me real joy is
the experience of being fully
engaged in whatever I'm doing.

Phil Jackson

If you don't know where you
are going, you are probably going
to end up somewhere else.

Laurence J. Peter

Don't confuse having a

career with having a life.

HILLARY CLINTON

Success is the child of audacity.

BENJAMIN DISRAELI

Don't find fault. Find a remedy.

HENRY FORD

Careers, like rockets, don't
always take off on schedule.
The key is to keep
working the engines.

GARY SINISE

Goodwill is the one and only asset that
competition cannot undersell or destroy.

MARSHALL FIELD

Talk to people in their own language.
If you do it well, they'll say, "God,
he said exactly what I was thinking."
And when they begin to respect you,
they'll follow you to the death.

LEE IACOCCA

For me life is continuously being
hungry. The meaning of life is not simply
to exist, to survive, but to move ahead, to
go up, to achieve, to conquer.

ARNOLD SCHWARZENEGGER

The individual who wants to reach the top in business must appreciate the might and force of habit. He must be quick to break those habits that can break him—and hasten to adopt those practices that will become the habits that help him achieve the success he desires.

J. PAUL GETTY

■ ■ ■ ■ ■ ■ ■ ■

I learned that the only way you're going to get anywhere in life is to work hard at it. Whether you're a musician, a writer, an athlete, or a businessman, there is no getting around it. If you do, you'll win. If you don't, you won't.

BRUCE JENNER

Making your mark on the world is hard. If it were easy, everybody would do it. But it's not. It takes **patience**, it takes **commitment**, and it comes with plenty of failure along the way. The real test is not whether you avoid this failure, because you won't. It's whether you let it harden or shame you into inaction, or whether you **learn** from it; whether you choose to **persevere**.

BARACK OBAMA

Every man's work, whether it be literature or music or pictures or architecture or anything else, is always a portrait of himself.

Elbert Hubbard

Ability is what you're capable of doing. Motivation determines what you do. Attitude determines how well you do it.

Lou Holtz

Life is not fair. Get used to it. . . . Be nice to nerds. Chances are you'll end up working for one.

Bill Gates

I remind myself every morning: Nothing I say this day will teach me anything. So if I'm going to learn, I must do it by listening.

Larry King

We are not people who believe only
in the survival of the fittest. Work in
America is more than a paycheck; it is a
source of pride, self-reliance, and identity.

JOHN MCCAIN

The most important single
ingredient in the formula
of success is knowing how
to get along with people.

THEODORE ROOSEVELT

All you've got to do is own up
to your ignorance honestly, and you'll
find people who are eager to fill
your head with information.

WALT DISNEY

Fall down, make a mess, break
something occasionally. And remember
that the story is never over.

CONAN O'BRIEN

If I miss a day of practice, I know it. If I miss two days, my manager knows it. If I miss three days, my audience knows it.

ANDRÉ PREVIN

Analyzing what you haven't got as well as what you have is a necessary ingredient of a career.

ORISON SWETT MARDEN

You've got to give loyalty down, if you want loyalty up.

DONALD T. REGAN

In the business world, the
rearview mirror is always clearer
than the windshield.

Warren Buffett

The worst days of those who enjoy
what they do, are better than the
best days of those who don't.

E. James Rohn

If you cannot work with love but
only with distaste, it is better
that you should leave your work.

Kahlil Gibran

Decide what you want, decide what you
are willing to exchange for it. Establish
your priorities and go to work.

H. L. Hunt

Keep your dreams alive. Understand to achieve anything requires faith and belief in yourself, vision, hard work, determination, and dedication. Remember all things are possible for those who believe.

GAIL DEVERS

■ ■ ■ ■ ■ ■ ■ ■

If there is any one secret of success, it lies in the ability to get the other person's point of view and see things from that person's angle as well as from your own.

HENRY FORD

I do not deny that many appear to
have succeeded in a material way by
cutting corners and by manipulating
associates, both in their professional
and in their personal lives. But material
success is possible in this world
and far more satisfying when it
comes without exploiting others.

ALAN GREENSPAN

The men who try to do something and fail are infinitely better than those who try to do nothing and succeed.

LLOYD JONES

Leadership and learning are indispensable to each other.

JOHN F. KENNEDY

A leader takes people where they want to go. A great leader takes people where they don't necessarily want to go but ought to be.

ROSALYNN CARTER

Making mistakes simply means you are learning faster.

WESTON H. AGOR

Don't limit yourself. Many people
limit themselves to what they
think they can do. You can go as far
as your mind lets you. What you
believe, remember, you can achieve.

Mary Kay Ash

■ ■ ■ ■ ■ ■ ■ ■

You've achieved success in
your field when you don't
know whether what you're
doing is work or play.

Warren Beatty

■ ■ ■ ■ ■ ■ ■ ■

Ability is of little account
without opportunity.

Lucille Ball

Enthusiasm is one of the most powerful engines of success. When you do a thing, do it with all your might. Put your whole soul into it. Stamp it with your own personality. Be active, be energetic and faithful, and you will accomplish your object. Nothing great was ever achieved without enthusiasm.

RALPH WALDO EMERSON

There are a lot of things that
go into creating success. I don't like
to do just the things I like to do. I like
to do things that cause the company
to succeed. I don't spend a lot
of time doing my favorite activities.

MICHAEL DELL

People who are unable to
motivate themselves must be
content with mediocrity, no
matter how impressive their
other talents.

ANDREW CARNEGIE

No executive has ever suffered because his
subordinates were strong and effective.

PETER DRUCKER

What great changes have
not been ambitious?

MELINDA GATES

First make it run, then make it run fast.

BRIAN KERNIGHAN

The toughest thing about success
is that you've got to keep
on being a success.

IRVING BERLIN

The price of greatness is responsibility.

WINSTON CHURCHILL

Above all, remember: You are not your resume. External measures won't repair you. Money won't fix you. Applause, celebrity, no number of victories will do it. The only honor that counts is that which you earn and that which you bestow. Honor yourself.

DOUG MARLETTE

I have never won anything without hard labor and the exercise of my good judgment and careful planning and working long in advance.

THEODORE ROOSEVELT

The supreme quality for leadership is unquestionably Integrity. Without it, no real success is possible, no matter whether it is on a section gang, a football field, in the army, or in an office.

DWIGHT D. EISENHOWER

Jumping at several small opportunities may get us there more quickly than waiting for one big one to come along.

HUGH ALLEN

A person knows when it just seems to feel right to them. Listen to your heart.

JOHNNY CASH

The person who starts out simply with the idea of getting rich won't succeed; you must have a larger ambition. There is no mystery in business success. If you do each day's task successfully, and stay faithfully within these natural operations of commercial laws which I talk so much about, and keep your head clear, you will come out all right.

JOHN D. ROCKEFELLER

My whole career can be summed up
with "Ignorance is bliss." When you
do not know better, you do not
really worry about failing.

JEFF FOXWORTHY

■ ■ ■ ■ ■ ■ ■ ■

Opportunity is missed by most
people because it is dressed in
overalls and looks like work.

THOMAS EDISON

■ ■ ■ ■ ■ ■ ■ ■

If the career you have chosen has
some unexpected inconvenience,
console yourself by reflecting that
no career is without them.

JANE FONDA

If you see a need, do not ask why doesn't somebody do something, ask why don't I do something. Hard work and persistence and initiative are still the non-magic carpets to success for most of us.

MARIAN WRIGHT EDELMAN

◼ ◼ ◼ ◼ ◼ ◼ ◼ ◼

The consumer isn't a moron; she is your wife. You insult her intelligence if you assume that a mere slogan and a few vapid adjectives will persuade her to buy anything. She wants all the information you can give her.

DAVID OGILVY

Big jobs usually go to the
men who prove their ability
to outgrow small ones.

RALPH WALDO EMERSON

Work while you have the light.
You are responsible for the talent
that has been entrusted to you.

HENRI FRÉDÉRIC AMIEL

I would rather hire a man
with enthusiasm, than a man
who knows everything.

JOHN D. ROCKEFELLER

Don't let the fear of striking out
hold you back.

BABE RUTH

A successful man is one who can
lay a firm foundation with the bricks
others have thrown at him.

DAVID BRINKLEY

Very few of the great
leaders ever get through
their careers without failing,
sometimes dramatically.

PHILIP CROSBY

The measure of success is not whether
you have a tough problem to deal
with, but whether it is the same
problem you had last year.

JOHN FOSTER DULLES

We measure the strength of our economy not by the number of billionaires we have or the profits of the Fortune 500, but by whether someone with a good idea can take a risk and start a new business, or whether the waitress who lives on tips can take a day off to look after a sick kid without losing her job—an economy that honors the dignity of work.

BARACK OBAMA

Success in business requires training and discipline and hard work. But if you're not frightened by these things, the opportunities are just as great today as they ever were.

DAVID ROCKEFELLER

■ ■ ■ ■ ■ ■ ■ ■

Leaders are made, they are not born. They are made by hard effort, which is the price which all of us must pay to achieve any goal that is worthwhile.

VINCE LOMBARDI

Skill and confidence are
an unconquered army.

GEORGE HERBERT

There is a kind of victory in good work,
no matter how humble.

JACK KEMP

Regardless of the changes
in technology, the market for
well-crafted messages will
always have an audience.

STEVE BURNETT

Customer satisfaction is achieved when
you sell merchandise that doesn't come
back to a customer that does.

STANLEY MARCUS

The miracle, or the power, that elevates
the few is to be found in their industry,
application, and perseverance under the
prompting of a brave, determined spirit.

MARK TWAIN

■ ■ ■ ■ ■ ■ ■ ■

Ability is sexless.

CHRISTABEL PANKHURST

■ ■ ■ ■ ■ ■ ■ ■

You cannot force ideas. Successful ideas
are the result of slow growth. Ideas do not
reach perfection in a day, no matter how
much study is put upon them.

ALEXANDER GRAHAM BELL

Nothing is interesting
if you're not interested.

HELEN MACLINNES

Leadership is the art of acomplishing
more than the science of
management says is possible.

COLIN POWELL

■ ■ ■ ■ ■ ■ ■ ■ ■

Good leadership consists of
showing average people how to
do the work of superior people.

JOHN D. ROCKEFELLER

■ ■ ■ ■ ■ ■ ■ ■ ■

Nothing happens unless first we dream.

CARL SANDBURG

The man who will use his skill and constructive imagination to see how much he can give for a dollar, instead of how little he can give for a dollar, is bound to succeed.

Henry Ford

To fulfill a dream, to be allowed to sweat over lonely labor, to be given a chance to create, is the meat and potatoes of life. The money is the gravy.

Bette Davis

So no matter how much potential you think you have, a little humility will serve you well—and help you focus on doing your best in the job you've got, rather than plotting to get the job you think you deserve.

KATIE COURIC

The future you see is
the future you get.

ROBERT ALLEN

The world is more malleable
than you think and it's waiting
for you to hammer it into shape.

BONO

Follow your passion, and
success will follow you.

ARTHUR BUDDHOLD

To succeed in business it is necessary to
make others see things as you see them.

ARISTOTLE ONASSIS

Leaders who win the respect of others are the ones who deliver more than they promise, not the ones who promise more than they can deliver.

MARK A. CLEMENT

The genius of communication is the ability to be both totally honest and totally kind at the same time.

JOHN POWELL

A leader has the vision and conviction that

a dream can be achieved. He inspires

the power and energy to get it done.

Ralph Lauren

Excellence demands competition.

Ronald Reagan

I suppose my formula might be: dream,
diversify, and never miss an angle.

Walt Disney

If you show people the
problems and you show
people the solutions they
will be moved to act.

Bill Gates

Failures are finger posts on
the road to achievement.

Charles Kettering

Work is a world apart from jobs. Work is the way you occupy your mind and hand and eye and whole body when they're informed by your imagination.

ALICE KOLLER

Ideas control the world.

JAMES GARFIELD

If I had eight hours to
chop down a tree, I'd spend
six sharpening my axe.

Abraham Lincoln

The successful person
makes a habit of doing what
the failing person doesn't like to do.

Thomas Edison

You have to have doubts.
I have collaborators I work with.
I listen and then I decide.
That's how it works.

Giorgio Armani

One important key to success is
self-confidence. An important key
to self-confidence is preparation.

Arthur Ashe

There are two kinds of people, those
who do the work and those who
take the credit. Try to be in the first
group; there is less competition there.

INDIRA GANDHI

Flash powder makes a more brilliant light than the arc lamp, but you can't use it to light your street corner because it doesn't last long enough. Stability is more essential to success than brilliancy.

RICHARD LLOYD JONES

■ ■ ■ ■ ■ ■ ■ ■

One of the tests of leadership is the ability to recognize a problem before it becomes an emergency.

ARNOLD GLASOW

■ ■ ■ ■ ■ ■ ■ ■

The man who complains about the way the ball bounces is likely to be the one who dropped it.

LOU HOLTZ

My experience has shown me that the people who are exceptionally good in business aren't so because of what they know but because of their insatiable need to know more.

MICHAEL GERBER

Nothing in this world can take the place of persistence. Talent will not; nothing is more common than unsuccessful people with talent. Genius will not; un-rewarded genius is almost a proverb.

CALVIN COOLIDGE

Don't give up. Don't lose hope.
Don't sell out.

CHRISTOPHER REEVE

■ ■ ■ ■ ■ ■ ■ ■

The difference between the
impossible and the possible lies
in a person's determination.

TOMMY LASORDA

■ ■ ■ ■ ■ ■ ■ ■

Don't be afraid to give up
the good to go for the great.

JOHN D. ROCKEFELLER

There is a fine line between
persistence and being straight out
annoying. Working someone's nerves
too much won't get you very far.

KATIE COURIC

I make progress by having people
around me who are smarter than
I am and listening to them. And I
assume that everyone is smarter
about something than I am.

HENRY J. KAISER

Always give a hundred percent,
and you'll never have
to second-guess yourself.

TOMMY JOHN

Anything's possible if you've
got enough nerve.

J. K. ROWLING

Success on any major scale requires you to accept responsibility . . . . In the final analysis, the one quality that all successful people have is the ability to take on responsibility.

MICHAEL KORDA

■ ■ ■ ■ ■ ■ ■

Mistakes are part of the game. It's how well you recover from them, that's the mark of a great player.

ALICE COOPER

No one can help you in holding a good job except Old Man You.

EDGAR WATSON HOWE

Happiness is the real sense of fulfillment that comes from hard work.

JOSEPH BARBARA

A brand for a company is like a reputation for a person. You earn reputation by trying to do hard things well.

JEFF BEZOS

Learn all you can from the mistakes of others. You won't have time to make them all yourself.

ALFRED SHEINWOLD

The critical ingredient is getting off your butt and doing something. It's as **simple** as that. A lot of people have **ideas**, but there are few who decide to do something about them **now**. Not tomorrow. Not next week. But **today**. The true entrepreneur is a doer, not a dreamer.

NOLAN BUSHNELL

It doesn't matter who you are,
where you come from. The ability to
triumph begins with you. Always.

OPRAH WINFREY

■ ■ ■ ■ ■ ■ ■ ■ ■

Many people worry so much
about managing their careers,
but rarely spend half that much
energy managing their LIVES. I
want to make my life, not just
my job, the best it can be.
The rest will work itself out.

REESE WITHERSPOON

■ ■ ■ ■ ■ ■ ■ ■ ■

Regard it as just as desirable to build a
chicken house as to build a cathedral.

FRANK LLOYD WRIGHT

I long to accomplish great and noble tasks, but it is my chief duty to accomplish humble tasks as though they were great and noble. The world is moved along, not only by the mighty shoves of its heroes, but also by the aggregate of the tiny pushes of each honest worker.

HELEN KELLER

The best work never was and never will be done for money.

JOHN RUSKIN

Don't bring negative to my door.

MAYA ANGELOU

Do a good job. You don't have to worry about the money; it will take care of itself. Just do your best work—then try to trump it.

WALT DISNEY

A pound of pluck is worth a ton of luck.

JAMES GARFIELD

All of the great leaders have had
one characteristic in common: it was
the willingness to confront unequivocally
the major anxiety of their people in
their time. This, and not much else,
is the essence of leadership.

JOHN KENNETH GALBRAITH

■ ■ ■ ■ ■ ■ ■ ■ ■

Achievement is not always success
while reputed failure often is. It is honest
endeavor, persistent effort to do the best
possible under any and all circumstances.

ORISON SWETT MARDEN

To **learn** through listening, practice it naively and actively. Naively means that you **listen** openly, ready to learn something, as opposed to listening defensively, ready to rebut. Listening **actively** means you acknowledge what you heard and **act** accordingly.

BETSY SANDERS

One measure of leadership
is the caliber of people who
choose to follow you.

Dennis A. Peer

Happiness lies not in the mere possession
of money; it lies in the joy of achievement,
in the thrill of creative effort.

Franklin D. Roosevelt

Learn to listen. Opportunity
could be knocking at your
door very softly.

Frank Tyger

It is easier to do a job right than
to explain why you didn't.

Martin Van Buren

In everyone's life, at some time, our inner fire goes out. It is then burst into flame by an encounter with another human being. We should all be thankful for those people who rekindle the inner spirit.

ALBERT SCHWEITZER

To be successful, you have to have your heart in your business, and your business in your heart.

THOMAS J. WATSON

People ask me all the time, they say to me, "What is the secret of success?" And I give them always the short version. I say, "Number one, come to America. Number two, work your butt off. And number three, marry a Kennedy."

ARNOLD SCHWARZENEGGER

NEVER TURN DOWN A JOB BECAUSE
YOU THINK IT'S TOO SMALL; YOU
NEVER KNOW WHERE IT MAY LEAD.

JULIA MORGAN

The question is not whether we
are able to change but whether
we are changing fast enough.

ANGELA MERKEL

DON'T SET COMPENSATION AS A GOAL.
FIND WORK YOU LIKE, AND THE
COMPENSATION WILL FOLLOW.

HARDING LAWRENCE

If you want to achieve excellence, you can get there today. As of this second, quit doing less-than-excellent work.

THOMAS J. WATSON

■ ■ ■ ■ ■ ■ ■ ■

Always be smarter than
the people who hire you.

LENA HORNE

Motivate them, train them,
care about them, and make winners
out of them . . . they'll treat the
customers right. And if customers are
treated right, they'll come back.

J. MARRIOTT JR.

The more I want to get
something done,
the less I call it work.

RICHARD BACH

Profit in business comes from
repeat customers, customers that
boast about your project or service,
and that bring friends with them.

W. EDWARDS DEMING

Men who never get carried
away should be.

MALCOLM FORBES

You win some, you lose some,
and some get rained out, but
you gotta suit up for them all.

J. ASKENBERG

Innovation distinguishes
between a leader and a follower.

STEVE JOBS

Big shots are only little shots
who keep shooting.

CHRISTOPHER MORLEY

Self-confidence is the key
to the universe.

CARROL WRACKLEY

You must never be satisfied
with success and you should
never be discouraged by failure.

RICHARD NIXON

A man to carry on a successful
business must have imagination.
He must see things as in a vision,
a dream of the whole thing.

CHARLES M SCHWAB

It's what you learn after you
know it all that counts.

JOHN WOODEN

Fear will keep you alive in a war. Fear will keep you alive in business. There's nothing wrong with being afraid at all.

NORMAN SCHWARZKOPF

Each indecision brings its own delays
and days are lost lamenting over lost
days . . . What you can do or think you
can do, begin it. For boldness has
magic, power, and genius in it.

JOHANN WOLFGANG VON GOETHE

It is a damn poor mind
that can think of only
one way to spell a word.

ANDREW JACKSON

We cannot direct the wind,
but we can adjust the sails.

DOLLY PARTON

Don't worry when you are not recognized,
but strive to be worthy of recognition.

ABRAHAM LINCOLN

Don't just work for the money . . . that
will bring only limited satisfaction.

KATHY IRELAND

Great work is done by people
who are not afraid to be great.

FERNANDO FLORES

It's not that I'm so smart, it's just
that I stay with problems longer.

ALBERT EINSTEIN

No man will make a great leader
who wants to do it all himself, or
to get all the credit for doing it.

ANDREW CARNEGIE

It's easy to make a buck. It's a lot
tougher to make a difference.

TOM BROKAW

The first requisite for success is the ability

to apply your physical and mental

energies to one problem incessantly

without growing weary.

Thomas Edison

You can't build a reputation on
what you are going to do.

HENRY FORD

∎ ∎ ∎ ∎ ∎ ∎ ∎ ∎

I have found no greater
satisfaction than achieving
success through honest dealing
and strict adherence to the view
that, for you to gain, those you
deal with should gain as well.

ALAN GREENSPAN

∎ ∎ ∎ ∎ ∎ ∎ ∎ ∎

THINK. Think about your
appearance, associations, actions,
ambitions, accomplishments.

THOMAS J. WATSON

When people go to work,
they shouldn't have to leave
their hearts at home.

BETTY BENDER

■ ■ ■ ■ ■ ■ ■ ■

The tragedy in life doesn't lie in
not reaching your goal. The tragedy
lies in having no goal to reach.

BENJAMIN E MAYS

I like to tell people that all of our products
and business will go through three phases.
There's vision, patience, and execution.

STEVE BALLMER

■ ■ ■ ■ ■ ■ ■ ■

There is no future in any job.
The future lies in the
man who holds the job.

GEORGE CRANE

■ ■ ■ ■ ■ ■ ■ ■

The way to get started is to
quit talking and begin doing.

WALT DISNEY

If you work just for money, you'll
never make it, but if you love what
you're doing and you always put the
customer first, success will be yours.

Ray Kroc

Never work just for money or for power. They won't save your soul or help you sleep at night.

MARIAN WRIGHT EDELMAN

Golf without bunkers and hazards would be tame and monotonous. So would life.

B. C. FORBES

Obstacles are those frightful things you see when you take your eyes off your goal.

HENRY FORD

Problems are only opportunities in work clothes.

HENRY J. KAISER

Use what talent you possess: the woods would be very silent if no birds sang except those that sang best.

HENRY VAN DYKE

■ ■ ■ ■ ■ ■ ■ ■

Desire! That's the one secret of every man's career. Not education. Not being born with hidden talents. Desire.

BOBBY UNSER

Even though quality cannot
be defined, you know
what quality is.

ROBERT M. PIRSIG

Success, the real success, does
not depend upon the position you
hold but upon how you carry
yourself in that position.

THEODORE ROOSEVELT

The test of a vocation is the love
of the drudgery it involves.

LOGAN PEARSALL SMITH

Outstanding leaders go out of their way
to boost the self-esteem of their
personnel. If people believe in themselves,
it's amazing what they can accomplish.

SAM WALTON

The big secret in life is that there is no

big secret. Whatever your goal, you

can get there if you're willing to work.

OPRAH WINFREY

A friendship founded on business
is a good deal better than a
business founded on friendship.

JOHN D. ROCKEFELLER

Remember the difference between
a boss and a leader. A boss says, Go!
A leader says, Let's go!

E. M. KELLY

Whenever you fall,
pick something up.

OSWALD AVERY

The manager accepts the status quo;
the leader challenges it.

WARREN BENNIS

Leadership is a matter of having people look at you and gain confidence, seeing how you react. If you're in control, they're in control.

TOM LANDRY

The will to win, the desire to succeed, the urge to reach your full potential . . . these are the keys that will unlock the door to personal excellence.

EDDIE ROBINSON

The purpose of life is
a life of purpose.

ROBERT BYRNE

Remember, America: organization
will set you free.

ALTON BROWN

The significant problems we face
cannot be solved at the same
level of thinking we were at
when we created them.

ALBERT EINSTEIN

Remember that time is money.

BEN FRANKLIN

Don't show off every day, or you'll stop surprising people. There must always be some **novelty** left over. The person who displays a little more of it each day keeps up **expectations**, and no one ever discovers the limits of his talent.

BALTASAR GRACIÁN

Happiness: the full use of your powers
along the lines of excellence.

JOHN F. KENNEDY

The difference between
intelligence and education
is this: intelligence will
make you a good living.

CHARLES F. KETTERING

Leadership: the art of getting someone
else to do something you want done
because he wants to do it.

DWIGHT D. EISENHOWER

Hard work spotlights the character
of people: some turn up their sleeves,
some turn up their noses, and some
don't turn up at all.

SAM EWING

■ ■ ■ ■ ■ ■ ■

It has been my observation that most
people get ahead during the time
that others waste time.

HENRY FORD

The ability to express an idea
is well nigh as important
as the idea itself.

BERNARD M. BARUCH

A business has to be involving,
it has to be fun, and it has to exercise
your creative instincts.

RICHARD BRANSON

Few people even scratch
the surface, much less
exhaust the contemplation
of their own experience.

RANDOLPH BOURNE

Leaders need to be optimists.
Their vision is beyond the present.

RUDY GIULIANI

We should be **careful** to get out of an experience only the **wisdom** that is in it—and stop there; lest we be like the cat that sits down on a hot stove-lid. She will never sit down on a hot stove-lid again—and that is well; but also she will never sit down on a cold one anymore.

MARK TWAIN

Don't bunt. Aim out of the ballpark.
Aim for the company of immortals.

DAVID OGILVY

■ ■ ■ ■ ■ ■ ■ ■ ■

Selling out is usually more a
matter of buying in. Sell out,
and you're really buying
into someone else's system of
values, rules, and rewards.

BILL WATERSON

■ ■ ■ ■ ■ ■ ■ ■ ■

Associate yourself with people
of good quality, for it is better
to be alone than in bad company.

BOOKER T. WASHINGTON

Nothing so conclusively proves a man's ability to lead others as what he does from day to day to lead himself.

THOMAS J. WATSON

The individual activity of one man with backbone will do more than a thousand men with a mere wishbone.

WILLIAM J. H. BOETCKER

A good plan today is better than
a perfect plan tomorrow.

GEORGE S. PATTON

I know the price of success: dedication,
hard work, and an unremitting devotion
to the things you want to see happen.

FRANK LLOYD WRIGHT

Leadership is, among other
things, the ability to inflict pain
and get away with it—short-term
pain for long-term gain.

GEORGE WILL

If I have a thousand ideas and only one
turns out to be good, I am satisfied.

ALFRED NOBEL

Success is not a destination that
you ever reach. Success is
the quality of your journey.

JENNIFER JAMES

Try again. Fail again. Fail better.

SAMUEL BECKETT

Don't keep forever on the public road. Leave the beaten track behind occasionally and dive into the woods. Every time you do you will be certain to find something you have never seen before.

ALEXANDER GRAHAM BELL

The three great essentials
to achieve anything worthwhile
are, first, hard work; second,
stick-to-itiveness; third, common sense.

THOMAS EDISON

Sometimes when you innovate,
you make mistakes. It is best to admit
them quickly, and get on with improving
your other innovations.

STEVE JOBS

■ ■ ■ ■ ■ ■ ■ ■

I have always loved the competitive forces
in this business. You know I certainly have
meetings where I spur people on by
saying, "Hey, we can do better than this.
How come we are not out ahead on that?"
That's what keeps my job one of the most
interesting in the world.

BILL GATES

Many of life's failures are people
who did not realize how close they
were to success when they gave up.

THOMAS EDISON

If the power to do hard work
is not talent, it is the best
possible substitute for it.

JAMES A. GARFIELD

Hard work without talent is a shame, but
talent without hard work is a tragedy.

ROBERT HALF

Real success is finding
your lifework in the work
that you love.

DAVID MCCULLOUGH

When all think alike,
then no one is thinking.

WALTER LIPPMAN

Your **profession** is not what brings home your paycheck. Your profession is what you were put on earth to do. With such **passion** and such **intensity** that it becomes spiritual in **calling**.

Vincent van Gogh

Don't let your ego get too close to your position, so that if your position gets shot down, your ego doesn't go with it.

COLIN POWELL

■ ■ ■ ■ ■ ■ ■ ■

Opportunities multiply as they are seized.

SUN TZU

Flying off the handle sometimes causes
hammers and humans to lose their
heads, as well as their effectiveness.

WILLIAM ARTHUR WARD

The winner is the chef
who takes the same ingredients
as everyone else and
produces the best results.

EDWARD DE BONO

Striving for success without
hard work is like trying to harvest
where you haven't planted.

DAVID BLY

Business life, whether among ourselves or with other people, is ever a sharp struggle for success. It will be none the less so in the future. Without competition we would be clinging to the clumsy antiquated processes of farming and manufacture and the methods of business of long ago, and the twentieth would be no further advanced than the eighteenth century.

WILLIAM MCKINLEY

■ ■ ■ ■ ■ ■ ■ ■

A business that makes nothing but money is a poor business.

HENRY FORD

Do what you love. When you
love your work, you become
the best worker in the world.

URI GELLER

You've got to seize the opportunity
if it is presented to you.

CLIVE DAVIS

■ ■ ■ ■ ■ ■ ■ ■

The most serious mistakes
are not being made as a result
of wrong answers. The truly
dangerous thing is asking
the wrong question.

PETER DRUCKER

■ ■ ■ ■ ■ ■ ■ ■

Try not to become a man of success, but
rather try to become a man of value.

ALBERT EINSTEIN

Focusing your life solely on making a buck shows a certain poverty of ambition. It asks too little of yourself. Because it's only when you hitch your wagon to something larger than yourself that you realize your true potential.

BARACK OBAMA

All growth depends upon activity. There is no development physically or intellectually without effort, and effort means work.

CALVIN COOLIDGE

It seems to me, that it's all about
opportunity and "make your own luck."
You study the most successful people, and
they work hard, and they take advantage
of opportunities that come that they don't
know are going to happen to them.

ERIC SCHMIDT

Respect a man,
he will do the more.

JAMES HOWELL

Leadership has a harder job
to do than just choose sides.
It must bring sides together.

JESSE JACKSON

Thankfully, perseverance is a good substitute for talent.

STEVE MARTIN

■ ■ ■ ■ ■ ■ ■ ■

I do not know anyone who has got to the top without hard work. That is the recipe. It will not always get you to the top, but should get you pretty near.

MARGARET THATCHER

Be willing to make decisions.
That's the most important quality in a
good leader. Don't fall victim to
what I call the "ready-aim-aim-aim-aim
syndrome". You must be willing to fire.

T. BOONE PICKENS

There are no such things as limits to
growth, because there are no limits
on the human capacity for intelligence,
imagination, and wonder.

RONALD REAGAN

You got to like your work.
You have got to like what
you are doing, you have got to
be doing something worthwhile
so you can like it—because it is
worthwhile, that it makes a
difference, don't you see?

HARLAND SANDERS

Never try to solve all the problems at once—
make them line up for you one-by-one.

RICHARD SLOMA

Don't let anyone else take the measure
of your worth and capabilities.
Always stand proud in who you are!

MARGARET SPELLINGS

It is amazing what you can accomplish
if you do not care who gets the credit.

HARRY S. TRUMAN

People are always good
company when they are doing
what they really enjoy.

SAMUEL BUTLER

Wise are those who learn that
the bottom line doesn't always
have to be their top priority.

WILLIAM ARTHUR WARD

Being good in business is the
most fascinating kind of art.
Making money is art and
working is art and good
business is the best art.

ANDY WARHOL

You know you are on the road
to success if you would do your job,
and not be paid for it.

OPRAH WINFREY

If you're in the luckiest 1 percent
of humanity, you owe it to
the rest of humanity to think
about the other 99 percent.

WARREN BUFFETT

There's nothing like biting off more than you can chew, and then chewing anyway.

MARK BURNETT

▪ ▪ ▪ ▪ ▪ ▪ ▪ ▪

Attitude is a little thing that makes a big difference.

WINSTON CHURCHILL

▪ ▪ ▪ ▪ ▪ ▪ ▪ ▪

We see our customers as invited guests to a party, and we are the hosts. It's our job every day to make every important aspect of the customer experience a little bit better.

JEFF BEZOS

You do not lead by hitting
people over the head—that's
assault, not leadership.

Dwight D. Eisenhower

Ability will never catch up
with the demand for it.

Malcolm Forbes

Half-finished work generally
proves to be labor lost.

Abraham Lincoln

There are no secrets to success.
It is the result of preparation,
hard work, and learning from failure.

Colin Powell

If you want to succeed you should strike out on new paths rather than travel the worn paths of accepted success.

John D. Rockefeller

■ ■ ■ ■ ■ ■ ■ ■

If people are coming to work excited . . . if they're making mistakes freely and fearlessly, if they're having fun . . . if they're concentrating doing things, rather than preparing reports and going to meetings—then somewhere you have leaders.

Robert Townsend

The real source of wealth and capital in

this new era is not material things . . .

it is the human mind, the human spirit,

the human imagination, and our

faith in the future.

STEVE JOBS

Nobody can be successful
unless he loves his work.

DAVID SARNOFF

■ ■ ■ ■ ■ ■ ■ ■

You can employ men and hire
hands to work for you, but
you must win their hearts to
have them work with you.

MERLE SHAIN

■ ■ ■ ■ ■ ■ ■ ■

An organization's ability to learn, and
translate that learning into action rapidly,
is the ultimate competitive advantage.

THOMAS J. WATSON

Real integrity is doing the right thing,

knowing that nobody's going to

know whether you did it or not.

Oprah Winfrey

If you're in a good profession, it's hard to get bored, because you're never finished—there will always be work you haven't done.

JULIA CHILD

· · · · · · · ·

Success is not a harbor but a voyage with its own perils to the spirit. The game of life is to come up a winner, to be a success, or to achieve what we set out to do.

RICHARD NIXON

In matters of principle, stand
like a rock; in matters of taste,
swim with the current.

THOMAS JEFFERSON

People who enjoy what they
are doing invariably do it well.

JOE GIBBS

Failure is the opportunity to
begin again, more intelligently.

HENRY FORD

Once you accept the fact that
you're not perfect, then you
develop some confidence.

ROSALYNN CARTER

When people are judged by merit, not connections, then the best and brightest can lead the country, people will work hard, and the entire economy will grow—everyone will benefit and more resources will be available for all, not just select groups.

BARACK OBAMA

To create a new standard, it takes something that's not just a little bit different; it takes something that's really new and really captures people's imagination.

BILL GATES

* * * * * * * *

The best executive is one who has sense enough to pick good people to do what he wants done, and self-restraint enough to keep from meddling with them while they do it.

THEODORE ROOSEVELT

Be different, stand out,

and work your butt off.

REBA MCENTIRE